Evidence of Being Here: Beginning in Havana
(N27)

Evidence of Being Here: Beginning in Havana (N27)

HANK LAZER

Negative Capability PRESS

ACKNOWLEDGMENTS

Thanks for the following editors & publications for publishing many of the poems in *Evidence of Being Here: Beginning in Havana (N27)*. The author is grateful for your support. And apologies from the author to any editors & journals that I forgot to acknowledge.

Plume (Daniel Lawless), *4ink7* (Russell Helms), *Lute & Drum* (Ken Taylor / Pete Moore), *Drunken Boat* (Ravi Shankar), *Negative Capability 33rd Anniversary Anthology* (Sue Walker), *VLAK* (Louis Armand), *Golden Handcuffs Review* (Lou Rowan), *Cold Front* (Nico Vassilakis) And thanks, as well, to Greg Randall for his invaluable assistance.

Evidence of Being Here: Beginning in Havana (N27)

Copyright © Hank Lazer, March 2018
Cover & Interior Design by Megan Cary
Library of Congress Control Number: 2017916068
ISBN: 978-0-9986777-2-9

Cover Notes: The cover image features a composite image of every page over-written on top of one another. Additional elements were created and incorporated from various pieces of public domain images available from NASA.

Negative Capability Press
62 Ridgelawn Drive East
Mobile, Alabama 36608
(251) 591-2922

www.negativecapabilitypress.org

For Lissa Wolsak

1/7/14
Havana

"sense takes on sense" <173>

"here we hear a place to begin" ... "unless an existence is the very provision by which something can ... one day ... hearing it begin" ... "beginning" ... "begin again" ... "'Transcendence' is the name we shall give to this movement by which existence transcends itself" <173>

1/10/14
Havana

layer upon layer
she calls & adds
a little more which
remains illegible no
way ever to know
for sure what is
meant by what is
said perhaps it is
merely the paying off
of a debt this
enigma of intent
& context perhaps
what we are
doing here cannot
be heard &
being here we
too are fully
enmeshed in the
inevitable difficulty
of this place

so who is playing whom for what & why

"Man is an historical species." L1747 & now a natural

to learn to listen to more carefully music as it permeates philosophy he said it was a "man insofar as he is a certain productivity." 1757

(after being quite sick i can return to think about other than my body's aches)

"in which economic relations are only effective insofar as they are lived and taken up by a human subject, that is, wrapped in ideological rags through a process of sense; it is, & that is exactly the way the world is & our being in it & in time & in our act of being and taken up by a human subject... in that we are not free to take much of it in at one go... then it is entertainment not art & we must rethink it... sort of... mystic fiction." <1763>

1/11/14
Havana

so he goes off to sea being this way he can stay alive of things no home no bed no steady fund for being the poetry of his daily returning home moon in many things i do not know or how to be standing what is standing on the balcony after our performance our improvisation there beside the Tao Te Ching i know that in the sudden downpour he calls us which is more important what you know or what you don't know

"It is said that sexuality is dramatic because we engage our whole personal life therein. But why precisely do we do this? Why else would our body be, for us, the mirror of our being, if not because it is a natural self, a given current of existence, such that we never know if the forces that carry us belong to us or belong to our body — or rather, are never entirely our body or entirely ours." ⟨174⟩

"of

traces

left

in us

by

words"

⟨179⟩

"Men can speak in the" the petition goes. "For me an electric lamp can become incandescent, but you are not writing." [1807] "you say you are writing, but you are not." [1807] "there is no one who speaks, there is not a soul, once you have read it & set it aside" where is this writing that occurs without any intention to speak governing it, be inscribed in the book of life, if, as the Tao says, perfect activity leaves no track behind — a way to open your own prompt, responding to a prompt.

1/12/14
Havana

(it was said to me
& I say it to you)

do not listen
as a trained musician
listen to what you are seeing here
until what you are seeing becomes a beckoned listening
(3) become the music of
a story of how
a beginning set of sounds
& a rhythm
& a rhyme
"thought does not accomplish anything" overheard
before it accomplishes a rhythm & a rhyme & a sense of
thought." (1821)

for ARD

he was a practicing hindu
& a poet a very good one &
a very speculative poet; so he was
rewarded in his next incarnation

he returned as an ashtray as
something of immediate practical use
to everyone — a sus ordenes — equally
beneficial to the smoker & the non-

now shall we make a list of the characteristics of everybody

"we do not have a thought on the margins of the text itself. The words occupy our entire mind" (05)

for OP

1/14/14
Tuscaloosa

our heart goes out to them

it is right here so we have a hard time

seeing it

leaving it

she carries herself well

"but we would not have been capable of predicting it and we are persuaded by it." 1857

1/17/14

"I relate to the word font from the way

; if in this way we are waiting

; if they may contact us ; if they are

; if this is the best way hand reaches for the place on my body being stung." 1877

; if you come to know it in the strange way it may be known in the ? way we have been given

rain down softly the traffic ? the vapor lane 1877

the light caress

1/20/14

in the waiting room
procession of the old & older
this invisible conveyor belt
crossing the bryant bridge
(the legendary coach retired & then died)
overlooking the Nucor plant
three plumes of white smoke rising into the clear winter air
the business of converting scrap metal into new steel
drafts caught in the updraft
book being written hidden from myself
"just as the only means the artist has of representing to ~~himself~~ herself the work ~~he~~ she is pursuing is by producing it" <1867>

(for RBD)

1/21/14

exit first

inevitable preface

looked

ever pointing toward

on mimetic suggestion

as a species in the universe we may constitute a dead end instance of unconquerable greed

that we will subsequently draw from it" <1887>

long hours on in everyday its opposite

and, on the first reading, a good read

i.e. inadequate unicorns

"a writer hardly ever rereads his own work

1/26/14

"But in fact every day

"according and gratitude for each

as it is there

the supposed spoken

as it is seen

silence became absent

as it is here

it's not noise is laughing

until you are able to feel

and words — "[68]"

... and we suffer within a world"

"Thought is nothing 'inner,' nor does it exist outside of words. What tricks us here, what makes us believe in a thought that could exist for itself prior to expression, is visions, are the already constituted and already expressed thoughts that we can silently recall to ourselves and by which we give ourselves the illusion of an inner life. But in fact, this supposed silence is buzzing with words—this inner life is an inner language." ⟨188-189⟩

"...words, sounds, and phenomena ... emanate from the voice box of this body in so many ways ... to shape a return from your ear ... i am thinking miracle ... singing the world." (1937). i often hear expressive sound waves

"or in which it modulates upon the keyboard of one form with another light, before again early morning as the cross over of acquired significations" with a deliberate act of breath. (1927)

1/28/14

woke to light

snow

who

or what

is

falling

now

it is sticking

ethics = gratitude

"The predominance of vowels & consonants in another... in one language;
several ways for the human body to confront the world one if finally
live it." 1937

1/31/14

"the intention to speak can only be found in an open experience of being; empty zones are constituted and move outward." <202>

a turning in gratitude in a more frequent sense of the miraculous that carries with it serious social consequences a passion for justice

what we are living as we are given these words for you please not merely mystification

2/1/14

"in order to once again throw itself beyond itself," "it is not what it is" <203> a new relation see for example the hundred or so not the beloved as remembered or expected behold fear "it is not where it is," it feeds "the enigmatic nature of one's own body" chipping sparrows pecking over the seed husks in a circle beneath the bird feeder

2/2/14

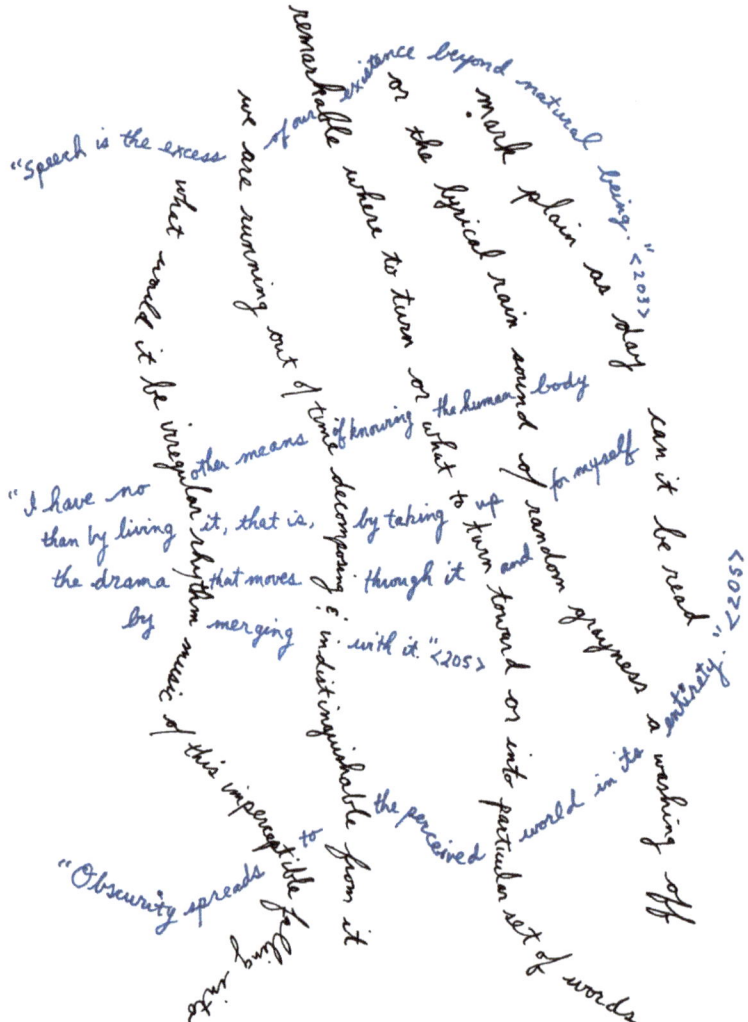

"Speech is the excess of our existence beyond natural being." <203>

mark plain as day can it be read or the lyrical rain sound of random grayness washing off remarkable where to turn on what for myself the human body can it be read in its entirety." <205>

we are running out of time decomposing & indistinguishable from it

"I have no other means of knowing the human body than by living it, that is, by taking up turn toward or into particular set of words the drama that moves through it and by merging music with it." <205>

"Obscurity spreads to the perceived world in its imperceptible falling into what would it be irregular rhythm

"...though, suddenly here... then I plunge into the thickness of the world." ⟨211⟩

perpetual experience

2/4/14

to see it — or first year detour to return to the simple art of seeing of now — what is it about this human seeing with complete "absolute seeing" life that requires a thirty it. to see it clearly I plunge into the "through perceptual experience thickness of the world." <???>

"and if the body is no longer a form is by taking it up, then rather an expressive unity that we can *solve* traction this structure will spread to the sensible world." ⟨213⟩

2/7/14

even Frost that cracker jack philosopher knows it is to be much

> ... The present
> Is too much for the senses,
> Too crowding, too confusing—
> Too present to imagine.

"truth little by little and never in its entirety"? <215>

the writing of it — the reading through which

perfectly explicit in front of us,

you ? i ? is in what senses

2/8/14

"...rather as a recreation or a reconstitution of the world at each moment" ⟨214⟩

the word
  the line
    the curve
      step down

that there is something
    to stand on

    that it is
      so very much
        like the page

  such is its nature

he cannot say the water never comes to a boil he is nodding off

"it is as if 'I' were never 'I', absolutely established against the background and upon the preparation of a pre-personal life of consciousness." ⟨216⟩

2/9/14

reconstituted each word being thought

"given that they are inwardly prepared"
"and sensation is literally a communion." (219)

"The perceiving subject is the place of these things, and the philosopher describes sensations and their substratum — as one might describe the fauna of a distant land — "so too we can discover a music-melody within a sound" [2.18] without noticing that he himself also perceives, that he is a perceiving subject, and that perception such as he lives it denies everything that he says about perception in general." 2.2 [4.7]

2/15/14

"Being only exists for someone who is capable of stepping back from it and is thus himself absolutely outside of being." 220

from here to there
are they messengers
a pointing toward
call it angel or word
a single letter
from there to here

my birth was like everyone else's: before my... is too with my death which in all truth dying rather place just like all that is "... not a mind." [222] But the life is [221] "... every sensation is a birth and a death." [223]

2/16/14

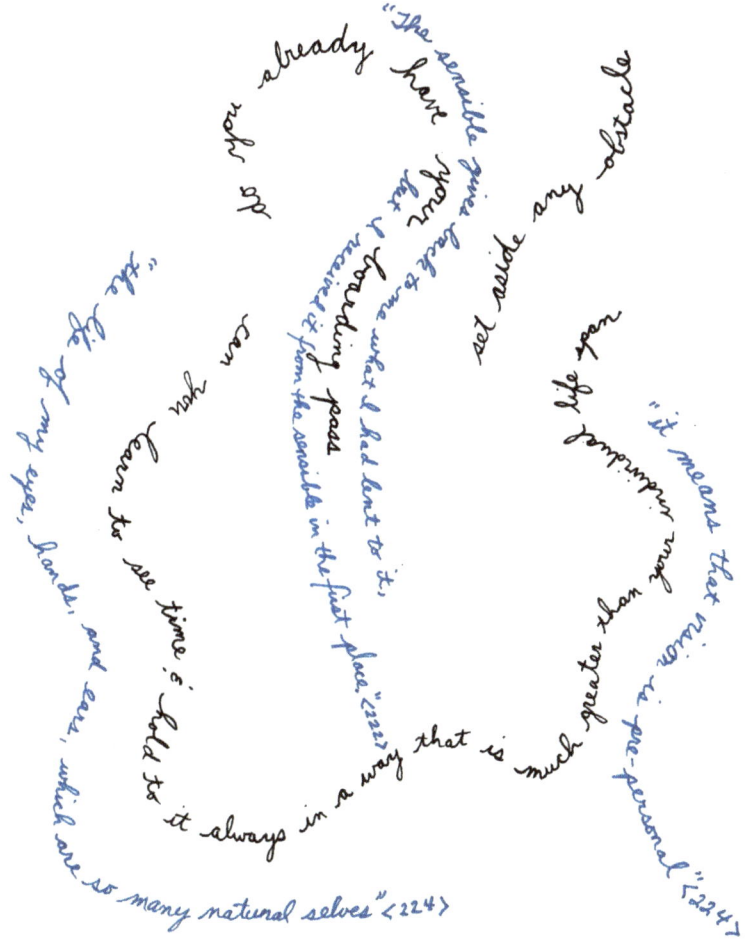

"The sensible gives back to me what I had lent to it, but I received it from the sensible in the first place." ⟨222⟩

"do you already have your span to see time's hold to it always in a way that is much greater than your life span" can you learn to "the life of my eyes, hands, and ears, which are so many natural selves" ⟨224⟩

set aside any obstacle

"it means that mine is pre-personal." ⟨224⟩

"I experience sensation as a modality of a general existence, already destined to a physical world, which flows through me without my being its author." <224>

"and from where do we learn that the world must be called so thought?" <227>

you must behold . i hold it hold everything . i think i have seen it wept

behold has nothing to do with holding or grasping

did you hear that i don't think we will ever know it once ; for all

2/17/14

"then the Pure Land is right here & when you find the right book it is very exciting for now i cannot remember exactly what i wrote yesterday it is still somewhere

"the primordial layer where Buddha's light is born: 'namu-amida-budsu.'" <12> KL

whenever you chant the name of the Buddha"

ideas and things are born." <228>

2/21/14

do
not
over
drama
tize

migration of souls

"Now, what does it

this place made for the trans

mean to focus...? <235>

"... or when I untie the link between my vision and the world or between myself and the world *roll over minutes* in order to catch it in the act and to describe it." <236>

2/22/14

...wander vaguely in front of the things, they have no place in the world, and suddenly they pull back toward a certain place in the world, less than the assembling of the soul are obeyed into the soul. "I am the ghosts return through the fissures of the earth from which they came when the day floods." <2142>

(i.) just as the memory images wander vaguely in front of the things are not given to all.) time is love & space is begin again — a summoning to — a summoning to — attention which is nothing more & nothing less than the assembling of the soul. (ii.) I think he told men who paint to make a stain or an image on the page all it takes to make them is the place we came to — pen and paper & the confidence to this place.

2/24/14

(he knew exactly what was happening) & refuses with comfort & this one now but is alive angry? asleep? wandering down the long corridor of dementia (2746) as they say his mind is mostly gone from all his studies. is this not the new purgatory? "...but the supposed..." when was it that he died (he was a neurosurgeon) (if you can afford it) with care

he would dissolve into his act and would have no consciousness at all *having any consciousness of himself* *perform, perform*

"If the thing itself were attained, it would from then on be stretched out before us without any mystery. What makes up the 'reality' of the thing is thus precisely what steals it from our possession. The acuity of the thing — its inexorable presence and the perpetual absence into which it withdraws — are two inseparable aspects of transcendence." ‹242›

about
face
so
just

simple

nothing

"... and because time escapes to the precise extent that it is grasped." ⟨2507⟩

no
mind
no
time

2/26/14

"how, nevertheless, this subjectivity is time itself... " day counting day praying day losing day mourning "... so we can follow Hegel in saying that time is the existence of the mind." "how we can turn into" morning beginning light day breathing ¿ am i still here ? it is friday, so i am reaching out to you

3/1/14

preparing to receive the word which is only a window on a vast room "Must we embrace the realm that, as Malebranche said, imagines the world going now or a destination or a dwelling place or as we live it now though then is now to renounce it though the idea and existing the objects in the world?" [251-2]

the sooner the better

pay him what you owe him

"when, breaking with the originary faith of perception, I adopt a critical attitude toward perception and wonder what I actually see..." <2517

"Nothing here it all says is thematized." <2517

hold down the compassion

as soon as i find myself thinking about the light simply that it is i wonder where is the compassion in that

"every perceptual act appears as taken from an overall adhesion to the world." <2517

she grew to look that way but not at first. "since space is anterior to its supposed parts," [253] "can you now when you tell me with any certainty what he or she is the face of another or how you feel fully what he or she will become what will be sequentially the means by which the position of things becomes possible," [253] "be achieved in time how that particular soul will be that body in time sometime you think you can see it & much less clearly how or rather, I said held of space at the moment," [254] "as I go for so," [254]

3/7/14

each sense of "The mere possession of a body brings with it the power of remembering itself, just as the possession of a voice brings with it in the face of the horror of the disease of forgetting namu amida butsu." <262>

early morning — an act of ritualized practiced meditation, a turn by daily deliberation, the taking up of a pre-personal tradition <265> — a counting oldies into accounting; a doorway into necessary self forgetting when acquired resolve is near; my personal existence must be "my history must be the...

"The spatial level is, then
 a
 but has no hold on the world." ⟨261⟩

as it was happening
i wouldn't call it the actual
certain possession of the world
 through
  each
 it was happening differently
yet has, a certain hold,

"that being is synonymous with being situated." ⟨263⟩
the wave you are riding
is called the dying
 of your body

"My body is wherever it has something to do." ⟨260⟩

3/8/14

light weight on the spring loaded feeder

a chickadee my little chickadee

this day a turning of the year or so it feels

i would turn but turn toward what — "appearing..." <265>

what is the weight of a soul

will it open or close the opening at the feeder food

"Space is neither an object... nor an act of connecting by the subject: one can neither observe it (given that it is presupposed in every observation), nor see it emerging from a constitutive operation (given that it is as for it to assume to be already constituted); and thus the clear spatial determinations bring brought into being can magically bestow space loaded feeder i know not the opening of

"Space is neither an object... at the feeder food"
"In order to reawaken perceptual experience" <267>

- 48 -

"We must gain access to a world through the *individual perspective, and by way of our return to nest the hidden it.*" [26.7]

evidence

of being here

scratched

on the page

mercy & compassion is that breaks & awakens you

"experience is either motion or..." (1147)

"breath is immediately transformed to life." (1747)

must it be suffering or it must be fatal." (2629)

"for God, info is everywhere."

ubiquitous as light

3/15/14

the sky has fallen touching moment of the perceptual faith in a unique thing." [274]

"and depth is nothing but a here where we are too

are you seeking never apparent ground unapparent

because god has attempts to see something. [274] clues by need i will never be certain

let it go to re-enter the miracle of this immediacy

"Depth is born before god has among

"Distance is immediately visible, provided we know how to find the living record which in fact is not a race for a writing that opens up a political motion it has constituted" <278>

where has that voice been this week as busy as we are hard then to see or live within this perfection is moving words to turn away

3/16/14

"There must be an internal relation between what is annihilated and what is born." (264)

if we relax & sit down beside them
let us listen in this restored cove
& relax with them in the continued severity of these considerations

enjoying friendship; enjoying this vast 1975 hp! summer evening; across different areas;

what do we make of this photo
the younger & older men
john ted & george
with their families

sitting on the gravelly shore beside sylvester's cove

stern consideration   a set of serious questions

3/22/14

arises the dawn beginning green

a voice fog haze ghostly gray infinite light

a calling an oddity intermittent to attune to

as water or the cold air of early morning

assuming you will sit with it ; let it come to you

behold is what the ark would be
bowl the empty space where being rests
below a turning to the calling voice

"Our visual field is not cut out of our objective world, it is not a fragment with well-defined borders like the landscape that is framed by the window. In the visual field we see just as far as the hold of our gaze upon the things extends — well beyond the zone of clear vision, and even behind ourselves." L289.7

- 54 -

3/23/14

JCF in Alamar

torture is visible up
on his face as
is the ecstasy that
on occasion visits him
he has stepped out
side of any typical
dailiness & is thus

most observant of each
day having within it
no routine for food
sleep no owned place
to be it is
a bright & painful
(he is there) light

"...reciprocally, what we do see is always, in some respect, not seen."

3/26/14

(circle, reading clockwise from top-left:) a thought permission returns; go back to zero which is here; is as free of intention as my heart beat or yours as the running of a

(center:) renew

"Thus my eye is never an object in perception." ⟨291⟩

3/28/14

quite curious

luminous burst

"do they touch

of human experience?" <300>

lyrical instant

quick wisdom   the contents

or something someone the

us

momentary   location

very structure of

a thin surrounding of

they say it's in your blood

consciousness,"

they or as they not merely give

heart beat & breath

not your life each with you

3/29/14

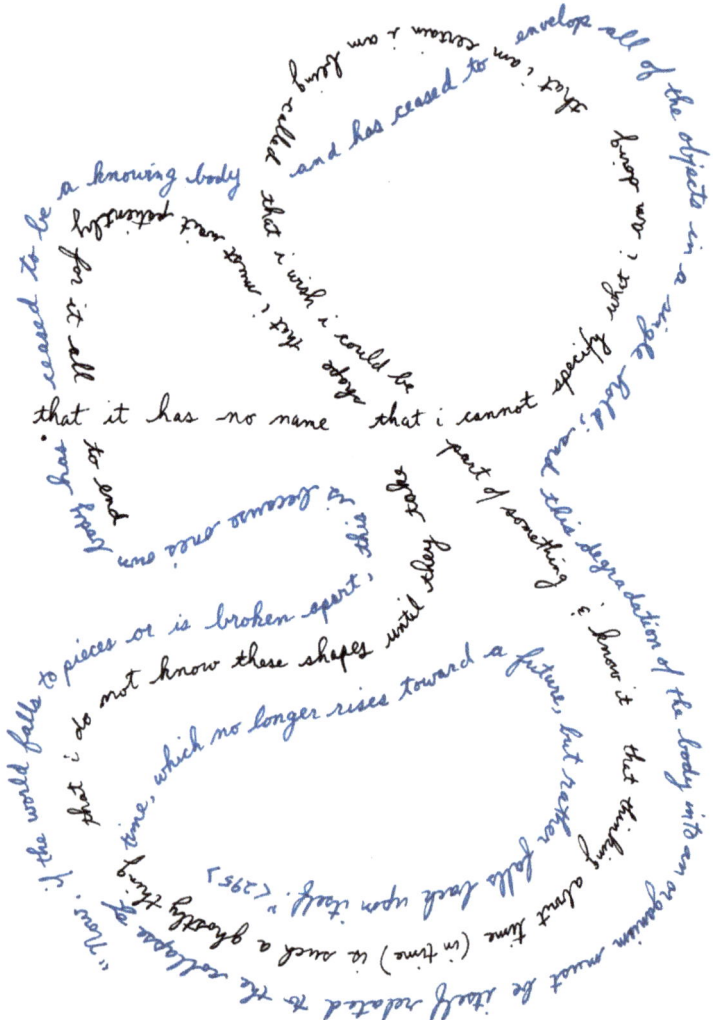

that i am a knowing body and has ceased to envelop all of the objects in a single field; and this degradation of the body into an organism must be itself related to the collapse of "now", the world falls to pieces or is broken apart, that i do not know these shapes until they take shape, which no longer rises toward a future, but rather falls back upon itself." (295)

"the future (in time) is such a ghostly thing" (295)

"the philosopher believes that he knows what he does better in reflection than he knows it in perception." ⟨302⟩

"we must keep at them." ... "learn from them."

"if we want to maintain a value for the testimony of consciousness" ⟨303⟩

sometimes this is all that we can do.

"he who does have some say in conveying fire is not the judge of what he fires." ⟨303⟩

4/1/14

i have written a wisdom book
lost in a larger book &
hidden from myself if i
would find it i
must do as you
would do i must
read it again &
listen to what it
is saying & then
shall we
extract it
or simply let it
remain hidden

[so?]: phenomenon, i.e., a word, phenomenon,
 to ask expression for it: our own.

i wish i could burst into flame & disappear

"... the world haunts us even in sleep, and we dream about the world <306>

till other voices wake

same
old
fool

us or we drown

4/4/14

arising from what

if each breath is a year

"m"

"And yet there is consciousness of something" [310]

4/5/14

the deeds smoothed over lost in the tangled complexity that allows *there is an absolute certainty of the world in general,* but not of any particular thing... necessarily, the hard look at the decisions at the face right of the governing greed *believe in a world* shamefully unequal distribution of the means to live "(31)". *to desire is to* a planet of radical injustice *pictures in the world...* shaped the page *o put our hand in* page the registration consciousness just ε, just to *have hurt of* for one interior for

4/8/14
Honolulu

"...there is an optimal distance from which

an occurrence in motion one of the sad marvels

finding momentary joy sitting still in a place

farthest on earth from other such places

it asks to be seen — an orientation

a notebook an island an edge a

gateway through which wind & tide & sun

through which we move toward transition

through which it provides man of itself — 3/6?"

finding momentary joy

new as she is to these conditions
the failing eyesight   the pooling fluids   the digestive anomalies
not yet determined energy
through the thickness of the world." <31>
counter measures   experimental sharpness
a way; a wave from memory a slippery or   have a
and at the same time united to them,
universe is herewith forced with   from its own being
"Consciousness is distant from being and
could turn back on its own way or so as if this
a mind so determined as to look the odds

4/10/14
diamond head

(circular text, reading around the loop): here what do you say within this flow of words when you hold your own

(blue text, extending outward): does not also increase / whether one's distance from them

they are turning in early
huddled within a simply made human cocoon
pressed against old brick buildings of chinatown

we walk through the humble human sleepers
as we return to our rental car
after a meal of innovative farm
to table vietnamese food

"less perfect in brief vision;
then in prolonged visions; that is"
<321>

"that is, to one..."
"keep him from ever more..." <321>

"determine things"

"the subordinate whole wig"

"our savored planet than our
of vanishing compassion"

"no longer are there any
wisdom at long distances" <322>

"no longer perceive invisible
space between each other" <321>

"lightness which stand out from each"

that place before name where being in consciousness

share the immortality lands of the simpler

4/12/14
diamond head

first light & its particular pain

to make (more) apparent each life,

the governing nothingness

emerging in time

this

from which

"we perceive according to light, just as in verbal communication we think according to ideas." [333]

"...then we suddenly have the impression of a magical lighting effect." [225]

(that comes from the virtues for the visible — ?)

4/13/14
diamond head

"But this can only be a manner of speaking, for we do not know our body or the power, weight and shape of its organs, like an engineer knows the machine he has assembled piece by piece." — page 7, bergson

planning or having a strategy
for when things get worse
a couple in their eighties
thinking rationally thinking proactively
where & near what & near whom
& the cost & how long & what
levels of care & sharing this
thinking with their children
while visiting together while
enjoying a thai meal in a
hole in the wall restaurant
in kaimuki not directly
a talk about death but rather
pleasure great pleasure and attention
to the almost perfect sauce
of the evil jungle prince

"...our perception is entirely sustained by the activity of the world." [326]

if god is
a singular
thing & we
gather together & aggregate · taking the light & the dark · finding a prior ground from which

4/16/14
Tuscaloosa

where or when will consciousness ever be at home

"It is not consciousness who touches or who palpates, it is the hand; and the hand is, as Kant says, 'man's outer brain.'"

4/18/14

"... that unique manner if i read it as its own book of existing." "it stands for frightening,

key: other voices

wake us

"afterwards"

or we

together over temporaneous, happier, different

given manner of being." <3337

sound of a glass expresses a single manner

4/19/14

flash

gold finches

:

indigo buntings

"The thing can never be separated from someone who perceives it... every perception is a communication or a communion." ⟨334⟩

"the unfolding of sensible givens
neither distance from them
nor affinity for them
beneath our gaze or beneath our hands is like
a language that teaches itself...
a temporary blossoming
witnessing a sudden seasonal color
within the dazzling light a mind
alights on nothing whatsoever
the thought soars infinite; it is the soul inhabits the body; it is not behind appearances." ⟨333⟩

4/21/14

nothing

can compare

with this

beautiful day

"...the miracle of the real world is that in it sense and existence are one, and that we see sense take its place in existence once and for all." <338> so we keep telling ourselves of course we matter

4/22/14

today's rain percussive fact

blossoms fall

from the dogwood tree

there is no organizing harbor
adequate to the infinite

the things, nor

particularity of this moment

or for that matter

of the process of fact

nor do we struggle to ...;

by secondarily do we notice the limits of our knowledge and of ourselves as knowing...?

4/24/14

a fence
is not
fool proof
either

sometimes the poem
is not enough to
sustain your presence
in the world

this power from its primordial attachment to the world itself". <34!>

denying itself in objective thought, and it draws

power that it has by this

what is a poem and what is the world

"Human life is already poetry

4/26/14

the descent

beckons

as the ascent

"Yet this is only the knowledge of things that varies. Almost unnoticeable upon my first glance, this knowledge is transformed into a unfolding of perception." ⟨342⟩

"The town I am approaching changes appearance, which I experience when I look at it again." ⟨344⟩ as I have just now a moment ago.

AFTER WORDS

Returning to N27 – Evidence of Being Here: Beginning in Havana

Returning to *N27* to see and think about what occurred, I note that the 27th Notebook continues and sustains (to my surprise) a writing project that began on October 8, 2006 (and that continues to this day – May 13, 2017, with Notebook 33). As the extended title for *N27* indicates, oddly, the initial writing project's focus – The Notebooks (of Being & Time), which began with a reading of and drawing upon Martin Heidegger's *Being & Time* – on an engagement with those amorphous terms *being* and *time* is fully a part of the writing that takes place from January 7, 2014 to April 26, 2014 for the 80 pages that constitute *Evidence of Being Here: Beginning in Havana*.

The notebook itself is small – 4" x 5 ½" – Ethiopian binding, with a cover image taken from a portion of deep space as seen through the Hubble telescope. (It could be a detailed section of light in a Turner painting…) And, as with Notebooks 21-30, the reading accompanying my writing is from Maurice Merleau-Ponty – in the case of *N27* specifically that great book *Phenomenology of Perception*. Perhaps what is most noteworthy about *N27* is that on page 19, and forever after, I began using the right color blue (principally for quoted material) – a wonderfully fine point, and a perfectly bright blue to contrast with the fine point black. So sorry it took me approximately 2,000 pages of writing/drawing and twenty-six notebooks to finally find the right blue.

The Notebooks, in partial retrospect, become a multi-faceted diary: part travelogue, part spiritual journey (jour as in day), a tracking of those elusive dimensions of being & time, a manifestation of momentary intervals of consciousness (in words & shapes), an improvisation at that time & place.

N27 begins with a fourth trip to Cuba, with soprano saxophonist/ composer Andrew Raffo Dewar, as we attempted to rectify an earlier experience where our jazz-poetry performance had to be canceled due to pressure applied by the state (Cuba). On this return trip, we were able to do two public performances, the latter with good friend Omar Pérez (poet, musician, artist, translator) who played percussion (on a handmade cajón). Thus, the first page marks an attempt to "begin again," in several senses: as each notebook is a beginning of sorts, as this trip began again our effort to perform the jazz-poetry improvisations. *N27*, on the first page, announces itself as a place to *hear* and be *here*.

As has happened throughout the notebooks – 1-10 drawing on Heidgger's *Being & Time,* 11-20 drawing on several books by Emmanuel Levinas, 21-30 drawing on several books by Merleau-Ponty, 31- to the present (N33) drawing on Dogen's *Shobo Genzo* – there is a fortuitous, chance-determined, coincidental rightness in the found quoted material. Merleau-Ponty's writings take on a strange, unexpected pertinence in the Cuban context: "man is an historical idea, not a natural species" and "… man insofar as he is a certain productivity."

This trip to Cuba also marked our last meeting with the great poet Juan Carlos Flores, whom I had met several years earlier in Alamar, a Havana suburb, and with whom we had rehearsed and improvised (at his Alamar apartment) a couple of years earlier when Juan Carlos was much healthier and more balanced. This visit, we met a spectral figure, a man who no longer had a home and who wandered around smoking cigarettes and occasionally eating. The ghostly Juan Carlos whom we met – sunken eyes, strange pronouncements – asked us which was more important, what you know or what you don't know. A year later, Juan Carlos committed suicide. His book – *Counter Punches* (translated by Kristin Dykstra, University of Alabama Press) – appeared a few months prior to his death.

The opening Cuba pages are infused with the specter of Juan Carlos, the success of our two concerts, and the humor of Omar Pérez.

As the twelfth page suggests, the Notebooks and *N27* specifically are a way to inquire – "& if this is the best way we can inquire   it is the way we have been given" – and, as the Merleau-Ponty quotations on the same page suggest, they are inquiries specific to how we *are* in this world: "I relate to the world just as my hand reaches for the place on my body being stung" and "… but rather an effort to reopen time."

In part, the reason for these reflections and this return to *N27* is that, as noted on page thirteen, the notebook is a "book being written hidden from myself." The Notebooks in general, and *N27* in particular, are writings that very quickly hide themselves from me, perhaps because of their distinctively momentary nature, their improvisatory (no draft) mode requiring an absolute immersion in their instance of creation. It is both a joy and an embarrassment to return to one's "own" work with such an element of surprise and unfamiliarity (though the text and I seem to warm up to one another fairly quickly). And the very next page of *N27*, in Merleau-Ponty's words, reminds me of an odd truth: "a writer hardly ever rereads his own works." Why is that, particularly since what we write exceeds any capacity of intentionality and will, and the re-reading (as with the writing of others) may provide an occasion for learning and additional thinking and questioning? Isn't it possible that the writing, reread, might contain something fresh, surprising, and worth reading? (If not, why expect someone else to care to read it!)

While *N27* participates in thinking about the relationship between words and thinking itself, perhaps the more important aspect of such consideration is to renew our sense of wonder at the kind of singing – the vowels, the phonemes – that is at the heart of our thinking and of our speaking to one another. The very music of our conversing (as nearly every page of *N27* consists of multiple voices and perspectives). Perhaps as *N27* makes evident, the repeated act of early morning meditation, *zazen*, is, for me, an important doorway for renewing that sense of wonder, and the shape-writing in the notebook provides and displays "evidence of being here   scratched on the page."

With the nineteenth page of *N27*, I finally settled on the "right" color of blue ink for my writing! More importantly, that page sets forth a fundamental realization and equation, putting forth the notion that ethics = gratitude. As this notebook reiterates, a training in gratitude and wonder must have consequences and actions in the external world (rather than remain a merely interiorized "treat" or "sweet" moment).

Often, in earlier Notebooks, the quoted material is only rarely in accord with or re-enforcing or deepening "my" writing. But in the case of N27, Merleau-Ponty's *Phenomenology of Perception* proves to be such a powerful educational force – not exactly a guide to my writing, but perhaps more like a star (or sun) about which the writing becomes an orbital instance. Merleau-Ponty points toward the complex and enigmatic nature of our life-in-a-body and our perceptual experience. He suggests, for example, "I have no other means of knowing the human body than by living it, that is, by taking up for myself the drama that moves through it and by merging with it." What resonates most for me – and the Notebooks are definitely a *hand*iwork, a thinking that bodies forth into unanticipated shape – is Merleau-Ponty's insistence on the enigmatic nature of bodily and perceptual experience – an experiencing that exceeds understanding (and that invites meditation). In the Notebooks, my life merges with the (momentary) writing of it, and with my immediate non-comprehension of it. Even so, the influence and guide that is always with me is the thinking of the poet George Oppen and his insistence on a deliberate seeking of clarity. (Indeed, Oppen's words echo throughout *N27*.)

"to what degree are we here now   you & i   & in what senses" constitutes perhaps the central questioning of N27. My greatest hope is that the book is sufficiently inviting that you will want to find out. That you will collaborate with, express, say, think with and about and through the writing. That you will find unanticipated ways to perform the pages*, thus re-animating them. "we can come to this place migrant to the page."

There is much more to say about *N27,* but at this point, I leave it to you.

May 2017
Tuscaloosa, Alabama

---

*In addition to the jazz-poetry improvisations performed with Andrew Raffo Dewar in Athens, Georgia, and in Havana, Cuba, see also three sound-pieces for N27P51 (3/15/14) – a collaborative project with Holland Hopson (in *Drunken Boat* #22: http://www.drunkenboat.com/db22/poetry/hank-lazer). There have also been noteworthy collaborative WORD EVENTS at The Grocery (Northport, AL), at Appalachian State University (especially of N27P50 – "mercy & compassion"), and at Notre Dame. When time permits during my poetry readings, I will work with audiences to create collaborative vocal/movement performances of a few notebook pages.

Praise for *Evidence of Being Here: Beginning in Havana (N27)*

In Hank Lazer's *Evidence of Being Here* philosophy and the lived present literally intersect. These poems are both concrete and metaphysical, open and dense. Here the general and the particular come together and dance.

—Rae Armantrout, author of *Partly: New and Selected Poems*

Hank Lazer's poems-in-motion are a kind expression of a *gay savoir*, a joyful wisdom, and if you're ever lucky enough to meet Hank himself, you'll think he's one of the tallest incarnations of a smart naive, a smiling white-haired head at the top of a six feet & something structure leaning on you with an almost ceremonial curiosity. But, beware, be aware for these structures he devises are as clever as they are childish: a connection with tides and winds, with tidal thoughts and windy recollections, is at work here, as if, in an energetic map of the world (that is, the human space), you could have a sinuous glimpse of a non-human capacity moving the hand, lubricating the brain.

Transcendence, Hank? Sure, but mainly ***transcendance*** of the pen-and-paper endeavor, in the nobility of a strenuous, and fun, exercise in the here & now; so, if ethics, as he says, equals gratitude, I find myself under the influence of a moral imperative to thank the poet and the word-fluids channeling themselves through his work and beyond.

—Omar Pérez, Cuban poet, author of *Algo de lo sagrado / Something of the Sacred*, translator of *Pensando Cantando / Thinking Singing*, musician, and friend to Walt and Emmie

Over a couple of decades Hank Lazer has been quietly and assiduously crafting one of the most eclectic and interesting bodies of work by an American poet. His serene and radical practice of atomic zoology, interactive reading and documentary observation has taken a turn to longhand lines written in field books he carries. The published results (in his original script) are collisions of insight that spiral off like the paths of quarks in a particle accelerator, liberated, fugitive, and blazingly destabilizing.

—Glenn Mott, author of *Analects on a Chinese Screen*, publisher at New Narrative Press

Lazer's notebooks speak to us in many languages simultaneously; enveloping readers as visual, theoretical, formal, philosophical, emotional, performative, and even musical texts, they are warm, open-ended and welcoming, while also being a recondite and exploratory 'reading through' of Merleau-Ponty, with many layers of meaning, interaction, and abstraction to discover anew via multiple readings.

—Andrew Raffo Dewar, saxophonist, composer, and ethnomusicologist

We were cruising down the road along Havana's Malecón. Next to me, Hank was writing things inside a notebook that fascinated me. I saw him writing in shapes, and to my surprise their structures were full of meaning, layers of language, the poetry as object, the notebook as object. At one point, out of the blue, he said:

> My grandfather fled to the United States from Russia. He was a Jew and escaped through China with his entire family. I was a little boy during the Cuban Missile Crisis. One night our whole family gathered to decide where we were going to move in order to escape nuclear radiation. I remember we decided to go to Australia.

On my way home, I remembered my fourth-grade classroom, during the Reagan era. One fine day they brought in an alarm, some artifact with three legs and a mythological name. The Siren. Then the bulldozers arrived and began to dig a shelter in the schoolyard. When the Siren went off, we would close our notebooks and climb down there, in the darkness, in silence.

*

Rodábamos por la Avenida del Malecón habanero; Hank a mi lado anotaba cosas en un cuaderno que yo miraba fascinado, escribía estructuras, que para mi sorpresa, estaban llenas de sentido, capas de lenguaje, la poesía como objeto, el cuaderno como objeto. En un momento, de la nada, me dijo:

> Mi abuelo llegó a Estados Unidos huyendo de Rusia, era judío y escapó a través de China con toda la familia. Yo era un niño cuando la crisis de los misiles. Una noche se reunió la familia entera para decidir a dónde nos íbamos a mudar para escapar de las radiaciones, recuerdo que decidimos irnos a Australia.

Volviendo a mi casa recordé mi aula de 4to grado en la primaria, eran los tiempos de Reagan. Un buen día trajeron una alarma, un artefacto de tres patas con nombre mitológico, La Sirena. Luego llegaron los buldóceres y empezaron a cavar en el patio de la escuela un refugio. Cuando sonaba La Sirena, cerrábamos las libretas y nos metíamos allá abajo, en la oscuridad, en silencio.

—Marcelo Morales, Cuban poet,
author of *El mundo como ser / The world as Presence*

In these wonderfully visual poems Hank Lazer lets language with its inherent capacity for investigation take us on multiple cartographic appearing expeditions. As we move through the pages – the maps – are activated by the spatial play of words up, down, across, between, through and over the resistances – both physical and mental – that his pen encounters while at work on the page. The sculptural volume and weight of the words inscribed in these curving arcs may well induce associations with the play of Alexander Calder's mobiles and/or the work of both modern and ancient earth works. With Lazer's work we have a mind, poet and artist carefully examining what it means to become alive through mobile constructions of language; what it means to leave traces; what it means to be physical while at the same time exploring what does it mean to make words become knowledge. Lazer's work is a beautiful and tenacious embodiment of that search and discovery.

—Stephen Vincent, Book Artist & Poet, most recently, *The Last 100 Days of the Presidency of Barack Obama, October 13 - January 20, 2017,* Drawings & Texts.

www.ingramcontent.com/pod-product-compliance
Lightning Source LLC
Chambersburg PA
CBHW061405160426
42811CB00114B/2378/J